SLANGUAGE
oetry from Dreamland

Peter Wuteh Vakunta

Langaa Research & Publishing CIG
Mankon, Bamenda

Publisher:
Langaa RPCIG
Langaa Research & Publishing Common Initiative Group
P.O. Box 902 Mankon
Bamenda
North West Region
Cameroon
Langaagrp@gmail.com
www.langaa-rpcig.net

Distributed in and outside N. America by African Books Collective
orders@africanbookscollective.com
www.africanbookscollective.com

ISBN-10: 9956-552-49-6

ISBN-13: 978-9956-552-49-8

Dedication

*In honor of Nelson Rolihlahla Mandela, South African freedom fighter
hailed for his ontological statement on the quintessential role of languages
in contemporary society:*

"If you talk to a man in a language he understands, that goes
to his head. If you talk to him in his language that goes to his
heart."

Table of Contents

Foreword

Poetry has the potential to serve as an antidote to societal ills, allowing the poet to work through issues in society, to find solutions to ontological mazes, seek clarity, provide solace to the sick in flesh and mind, and provide peace in times of turmoil. Versification provides a vehicle of expression for diverse attitudes, and fresh insights. Throughout life, from the cradle to the grave, we store information culled from our lived experiences; from the travails of others, and try in some way to make sense of it all. When we are in a conundrum and cannot find signification in the things that transpire in our lives, we attempt to externalize our inner musings through writing. A committed writer must be preoccupied with his time. He must address himself to the human predicament. True artistic endeavor shouldn't be confounded with ideological propaganda. Art for art's sake is an anachronism in a world beset with the pangs of diseases, oppression, illiteracy, genocides, ethnic bigotry, exploitation, neo-colonialism and imperialism.

The poems contained in *Slanguage (Poetry from Dreamland)* are cathartic songs. They convey an amalgam of experiences culled from the poet's peregrinations around the globe. Each poem translates an emotion. This anthology is the externalization of the poet's pent-up emotions, the vocalization of a piece of a mind that yearns to bring sanity to a world that has gone berserk.

"I have fought against white domination, and I have fought against black domination. I have cherished the ideal of a democratic and free society in which all persons will live together in harmony with equal opportunities. It is an ideal, which I hope to live for, and to see realized. But my Lord, if needs be, it is an ideal for which I am prepared to die."

[Nelson Mandela, defense statement during the Rivonia Trial, 1964. Also repeated during the closing of his speech delivered in Cape Town on the day he was released from prison 27 years later, on 11 February 1990]

Bush-Faller

Slanguage

What's this brouhaha
About alien accents?
Who the heck knows what you mean
When you say 'bubbler' for 'water fountain'?

What's this hullabaloo
About strange accents?
Who in the world knows what you mean
When you say 'trunk' for 'boot' of a car?

What's this raving and ranting
About foreign accents?
Which son of a gun knows what you mean
When you say 'betcha' for 'thank you'?

What's this rowdiness
About strong accents?
Who the hell knows what you mean
When you say 'pop' for 'soda' or 'soft drink'?

What's this humbug about
Bizarre accents?
Who on earth knows what you mean
When you say 'pants' for 'trousers'?

What's this hubbub?
About unusual accents?
Pray, who knows what you mean
When you say 'purse' for 'handbag'?

Need we really whine about
Communicative idiolects
When we're all so idiosyncratic
In our speech mannerisms?

Nomenclature

What's in a name?
There's nothing more important
Than a person's name.
Why then do we toy with names?
People no longer bear their real names!
We take liberties with other people's names:

Elizabeth has become Beth or Lisa,
Jennifer has been re-christened Jenny,
Susan has metamorphosed into Sue,
Patricia has been reborn Pat or Patti,
Christopher has been transformed into Chris;
Michael is Mike.

Charles is Chuck,
Henry is Hank,
Robert is Bob,
Emmanuel is Manu,
Samuel is Sammy,
Joseph is Joe.

James is Jim,
Thomas is Tom,
Bonaventure is Bon.
The list is not exhaustive.
Why are we doing this?
We make others feel like
human counterfeits!

Do you know what's done
to people who have tongue-twisting
Names like *tchokolokobangoshia*?
We ignore them altogether!
Isn't that smart?

People's names are their most
Valued gifts from birth.
We have no leeway to
trifle with nomenclature.

Docta

Quand je think about les doctas kamerunais
Je wanda que vraiment qu'est-ce qui
Ne va pas avec nos intellos?
Sont-ils tout simplement mboutoucous
Or bien ils ont carrément perdu la boussole?

Prenons le cas de ce fameux
Jacques Famé Ndongo qui se comporte
Comme un Johnny four-foot.
When he says silly things like:
Nous sommes tous les créatures de Paul Biya.

Que veut-il vraiment langua?
Does he mean that tous les Camers
Sont aussi mbout que Popol
Ou bien il veut tok que quoi?
Que les Camers sont tous membres
De la bande d'Ali Baba et les 40 mazembes?

Cheh, je vous dis que
Les intellos kamerunais
Vont nous faire voir de toutes les couleurs
Je dis bien de toutes les couleurs, hein!
C'est vrai que l'impossible n'est pas camerounais
Mais faut pas que les doctas abusent quand même!

Ici au mboa il y a les doctas kan kan:
Tu vas à Ngoa Ekelle,
Tu vas nyè les doctas qui fok
Les yoyettes sur le plancher dans leurs bureaux.

Ahan, n'oubliez pas le langua de deuxième bureau-o.

Tu vas à l'hôpital,
Tu verras les doctas qui nyoxent avec les malades
Croyez-moi mbombo! Pas de toli!
Ce que l'oeil nyè
La bouche ne peut pas refuser de langua.
Doctas dey for Ngola kind by kind.

Speak Right!

Speak truth!
Il est si beau de vous entendre
parler de Reunification of LRC and Southern Cameroons
ou du profil gracieux et élogieux
qui tremble dans les sonnets de René Djam Afame
Nous sommes un peuple inculte et bègue
mais ne sommes pas sourds au génie d'une langue
parlée avec l'accent de Samuel Minkio Bamba
et Moïse Nyatte Nko'o speak frankly
Et pardonnez-nous de n'avoir pour réponse
que les chants rauques de nos ancêtres
et le chagrin de Foumban

Speak truth!
Parlez des choses et d'autres
parlez-nous de Mount Mary
ou du monument à John Ngu Foncha
du charme gris des Grassfields
de l'eau rose du Wouri
parlez-nous des trahisons
nous sommes un peuple peu brillant
mais fort capable d'apprécier
toute l'importance des prévarications
 et des propos bidons et houleux
mais quand vous really speak truth

quand vous get down to the bottom of matters
pour parler du gracious living on both sides of the Mungo
et parler du standard de vie
et de la Grande Société ongolaise

un peu plus fort alors speak truth
haussez vos voix de maîtres
nous sommes un peu durs d'oreille
nous vivons trop près des machines
et n'entendons que notre souffle au-dessus des outils
Speak truth loud and clear!

Qu'on vous entende
de Bamenda à Mvo Meka en Camerounais
Oui quelle admirable langue
pour donner des ordres
Pour mater tout soulèvement
Pour fixer l'heure de la mort à l'ouvrage
et de la pause qui rafraîchit
et ravigote le Franc CFA
Speak truth!
Tell us that God is on vacation in Ongola
And that we're paid to trust him
Speak truth
Parlez-nous de production, profits et pourcentages
Speak truth
C'est une langue riche
Pour s'acheter
Mais aussi pour se vendre
Se vendre à perte d'âme

Speak truth!
Tu parles!
Mais pour vous dire
l'éternité d'un jour de Conférence Nationale Souveraine
pour raconter
une vie de peuple pris en otage
mais pour rentrer chez nous

à l'heure où le soleil s'en vient crever au-dessus des ruelles
mais pour vous dire que le soleil se couche
chaque jour de nos vies à l'est de vos empires
rien ne vaut une langue à jurons:
Anglos, ennemis dans la maison, Biafrais
notre parlure pas très propre
tachée de cambouis
Speak right!
Soyez à l'aise dans vos propos
Nous sommes un peuple rancunier
Mais ne reprochons à personne notre sort
d'avoir le monopole
de la correction de langage
Dans la langue douce de Shakespeare
avec l'accent de Bernard Fonlon
parlez un anglais pur et atrocement blanc
comme en Grande Bretagne
parlez un français impeccable comme en France
une étoile noire entre les dents
Parlez rappel à l'ordre
Parlez répression

Speak right!
c'est une langue universelle
nous sommes nés pour la comprendre
avec ses mots lacrymogènes
avec ses mots matraques
Speak truth
Tell us again about Freedom and Democracy
Nous savons que liberté est un mot noir
Comme l'émotion est nègre
et comme le sang se mêle à la poussière
des rues d'Abakwa ou de Molyko

Speak right!
de Garoua à Nkambe relayez-vous
Speak truth comme cela se doit
Speak truth comme dans l'Evangile
Be civilized!
Et comprenez notre parler de circonstance
quand vous nous demandez poliment
how do you do?
et nous entendez vous répondre
We're doing all right!
We're doing just fine
We are not alone, you know.
Je sais dans mon fort intérieur
que nous ne sommes pas seuls dans cette vendetta.

Power of the Word

In my village,
the *griots1* are truly revered.
They are the *maîtres de la parole2*,
Masters of the word.

In my homeland,
the gift of the gab is highly honored,
And aphorisms are the honey
with which words are eaten.

In my native-land,
a good orator eats the tastiest food,
and drinks the freshest palm-wine.

In my home-town,
a good storyteller marries
the sexiest woman,
and owns the most land.
Word of mouth,
It is magic!

---

1 Bard
2 Masters of the word

DREAMLAND

Uncle Sam

Uncle Sam is best qualified
By one epithet——freedom.
Uncle Sam is more than a mere
Geographical expression.
It is the land of the free.

And of the brave.
Home of institutionalized democracy;
And of equal rights.
Uncle Sam is more than a mere
Dream land--

Land of dream and prosperity
Flowing with milk and honey,
Dream of success;
Dream of strength,
Of global dominance.

Uncle Sam is more than a mere
Geographical expression—
Land where all persons regardless
Of race, gender, or ethnicity
Live in full communion.

American Dream

Hip! Hip! Hooray!
At the first it looked
Like a perfect optical illusion.
But then slowly and surely
Disbelief faded into certitude.
I had hit the green jackpot!

Uncle Sam beckons me.
This bodes well for my
Better half and progeny.
The journey to dreamland
Was no piece of cake.
I'd worked and toiled

Strong in my conviction
That where there's a will
There's always a way.
I had one gnawing ambition:
Set foot in Dreamland
And set up residence.

That which transpires
In due course was inconsequential.
What will be will be.
Qui vivra verra!
Man no die man no rotten[3]
What fate has in store

---

3 Nothing ventured, nothing gained.

Only time will tell.
God's time is the best.
God he court no get appeal.[4]
Huruje! Huruje! Huruje!
Kukum Kukum Massa!
Ooh!Kukum Kukum!

---

4 There is no appeal in God's Court of law

Jim Crow[5]

Jim Crow is dead
Long live Jim Crow!
Old habits diehard.

A leopard never loses its spots.
The requiem for Jim Crow
Was sung ages ago.
Yet Jim Crow lives!

How many times
Have you been labeled nitwit
For no other reason
But the color of your skin?

How too often have you been subjected
To less than human treatment
On account of the texture of your hair?

Have often have they branded
You subhuman in veiled terms
Owing to your ethnicity?

How many times have they deprived
You of a job opportunity because
Of your race?
Refraining from giving merit
Where merit is due.
Never mind Affirmative Action!

---

5 Practice or policy of segregating or discriminating against blacks.

Come to think of it,
Hate-mongers and Ku Klux Klan
Aren't dead and buried.
They've merely gone underground.

Mirage

Our insatiable thirst for war
Hangs on thinly veiled falsehoods:
The liberation of oppressed peoples
Is an act of magnanimity?
The fact of the matter is our warmongering
Has nothing to do with freedom.
It is about self-aggrandizement.

Dictators are a threat to
Global peace and us.
In fact, they are our worst enemies;
Aren't we dictatorial too?
The real threat to world peace is our unbridled
Desire to erect a Grand Empire.

Dictators ride back and forth on paper tigers
However, dare not descend
For fear of being devoured
By their own tigers!
They have ties with
International terrorists.
Dictators and terrorists are bedfellows.

Pheonix in Oval Office

Election America 2020—
Veritable vendetta!
I saw David pitted against Goliath,
I saw the clash of bigotry with magnanimity.
I saw the triumph of altruism over egocentrism.

Election America 2020—
I heard the raucous cacophony of an owl
Drown by the sweet lyrics of a phoenix.
I heard the debilitating rant of myopia
Muted by the melodious chant of perspicacity.

Election America 2020—
Merciless tug of war!
I saw indigence at daggers drawn with opulence.
I saw humility at loggerheads with superciliousness.
I saw veracity fighting tooth and nail against EVIL.

Election America 2020—
Cut-throat duel!
I smelt the triumph of Light over Darkness.
I sensed the victory of a Messiah
Over the Waterloo of Judas.

Election America 2020—
I witnessed the landslide of Majority over Minority.
I witnessed the triumph of Black over White.
Black and Proud!
Not the Wretched of the Earth anymore.

Election America 2020—
Never say never again!
Fools walk where angels
Dread to tread
Others live in fool's paradise.

Election America 2020—
Goliath reduced the Battle
To bread and butter,
David saw it as a civil rights matter—
America with liberty and justice for ALL!

Election America 2020—
From 'loser' to Winner!
From He that leads from behind
To Commander-in-Chief!
From Two-Term to One-Term President!

Election America 2020—
The chickens have come home to roost.
Hail! Hail Joe!
Long Live Joe!
Vive Joe B!

Dirty Linen

Photos of callous sexual assaults
at the Abu Ghraib Prison
perpetrated by our soldiers
reveal much about us as a nation.

Horrific scenes at Abu Ghraib
bring to mind the animalistic sexual
humiliation meted out on our military
women by men in uniform
at the Denver Post in bygone years.

The inhumanity manifested
at Abu Ghraib by stone-hearted soldiers
under the gleeful eyes
of the "thumbs-up"
Lyndie England is a replay of the
daily ordeal at the
infamous Guatanamo camp.

We may not know that we are
washing our dirty linen in public.
The fact of the matter is that
collectively we cut the picture
of an unclean nation.
We glorify sadism,
We reward megalomania,
We lie to ourselves constantly,
The world is simply sick and tired
Of our false pretenses!

PYRRHIC VICTORIES

Bayonet

Kill! Kill! Kill!
It's the spirit of the bayonet
Blood makes grass grow.
What makes grass green?
Blood! Blood! More blood!
Victory starts here!

Methinks ours is
But Pyrrhic victory—
One too costly to be of
Any real value to us.
We may know all our
Reassuring code-names:

Operation Infinite Justice;
Operation Enduring Justice;
Operation Just Cause;
Operation Desert Storm;
Operation Iraqi Freedom;

Alas,
We'll never know the names
Of all our compatriots,
Women and men,
Black and white,
Killed in the name of freedom.

Balls

I am a M.A.N
Je suis homme
Homme avec une barbe
I am a M.A.N
I refuse to cave in to the dictates of riff-raff

I am a M.A.N
Je suis homme
Homme avec un bangala
I am a M.A.N.
I dare not stoop down to inanities.

I am a M.A.N
Je suis homme
I am a Man
I will not kowtow to the machinations
Of benighted backstabbers.

I am a M.A.N
Je suis homme
I am a Man
I decline to give carte blanche
To servants of the green-eyed monster.

I am a M.A.N
Je suis homme
I am a Man
I know myself too well.
I rise above societal scum.

I am a M.A.N
Je suis homme
I am a Man
M.A.N
I dine not with the scumbags of society.

I am a M.A.N
Je suis homme
I am a M.A.N
I pay no heed to the ranting
Of scumbags of planet Earth.

Hades yes!
Putain! Je suis homme
Hell, yes!
I am a Man.
Trifles leave me unperturbed.

Leeway

This asteroid is screwed up!
I wanna say what I gotta say
No numskull's gonna
Tell me to shut up!
The underworld has put
every dick in dipshit.
This gives me the creeps.

This joint's gone bonkers!
Bunch of dirtballs have
hijacked no man's land
What do yo make of that?
Say they're slaughtering in God's!
That's a load of crap!
Yo shall not kill,
Is the first law in Holy Book!
Servants of Satan kill in God's name.

These dirt bags
are darned assholes
Say they're a cocky self-serving nation.
Cold fact is they're pissed
off at others' freedoms:
freedom to know, think and
worship according to their conscience.

Barrel of the Pen

He that cherishes peace;
Should prepare for war,
Quips the warmonger!
There goes the old wives' tale!

An armed nation is a safe nation.
Phoney admonitions to be taken
With a grain of salt.
Those who seek war scarcely know
They'll perish on the battlefield.

The mayhem wrecked
by gun-totting youngsters
in and around these precincts
attests to the folly that fuels
the craze for firearms.

Places of learning
transformed into war zones
Religious sanctuaries
converted into battlefields
by trigger-happy delinquents.
In every nook and corner,
the specter of death
hangs over our heads
like the proverbial
sword of Damocles.

The media has further
emboldened a great many folks

by churning out the hollow
propaganda according to which a gun-free
nation is perforce an unsafe nation.
That's a tall tale.

Bravado

I flex my muscles,
I prime my gun;
I pull the trigger
And fire fatal shots
Poom! Poom! Poom!

My foe drops dead
in a pool of blood.
Does that solve the problem?
Is there freedom in the casket?
Is there freedom to kill?

Humankind is deranged!
Very sick, indeed.
Do I have to annihilate
in order to build?
That's the modus operandi
of bellicose nations:
Building castles in the air!

I listen to the voice of reason
in the wilderness crying out for peace.
I want to go the way of pacifism,
War-mongering is nothing
but bravado in futility.

Same Boat

The same fate awaits all Men.
As one man dies, so does his brother;
Black men like white men.
All of us breathe the same air,
The same red blood runs through our veins.
We eat and drink alike;
We defecate in the same way;
And urinate in like manner.

In coitus,
We assume the same posture.
In childbirth,
We take the same skyward position.
No pigmentation is mightier
Than the other.
No woman has an edge
Over her sister before the Creator.

Before God, all men are equal.
From dust we came,
Unto dust we shall return.
There are no greater.
Or lesser human beings.
We are all in the same boat.

Food for Thought

When Papa passed on
I grieved.
Soon he'll be food for maggots.
So is George Washington!

When Mama was deceased
I cried.
Soon she'll be food for maggots.
So is Rosa Parks!

When grandpa died
I wept.
Soon he'll be food for maggots
So is Abraham Lincoln!

When grandma passed away
I lamented.
Soon she'll be food for maggots.
So is Mother Theresa!

When my brother gave up the ghost
I broke down.
Soon he'll be food for maggots.
So is Dr Martin Luther King!

When my sister departed
I mourned.
Soon she'll be food for maggots.
So is Harriet Tubman!

When my uncle expired
I sobbed.
Soon he'll be food for maggots
So is Malcolm X!

When my aunt left us
I moaned
Soon she'll be food for maggots.
So is Sojourner Truth!

When my cousin returned to dust
I sobbed,
Soon he'll be food for maggots.
So is Mahatma Gandhi.

When my nephew returned to his creator
I wept,
Soon he'll be food for maggots.
So is Ronald Reagan.

Slave or slave master,
Free or shackled,
Colonized or colonizer,
Black or white,
Rich or poor
Humble or conceited,
All food for maggots!

Makwerekwere Trumpeters

As pressure mounts on
The Azanian political elite
To fulfill the post-apartheid promises
Made to the rank and file,
The rest of world is taken aback
To learn that many Azanians of color
Regard Africans from other climes
Not as comrades in the liberation struggle,
But as 'makwerekwere'.

This derogatory epithet connotes
'Foreigners' perceived,
Wrongly or rightly, as job-snatchers and
Conveyors of communicable diseases.
It bears stressing that we need
Not overreact to this misconception.
The 'kwerekwere' trumpeters
Have been cut off from the rest
Of Africa and the world for far too long.
Many of us know a lot about them
But they don't know us one bit.
We must strive to build a bridge
Between knowledge and crass ignorance
In a fraternal fashion.

Summum Bonum

In keeping with social contract,
the good of each person
is linked to the common good.
It serves no purpose living
Like an island sufficient onto oneself
entirely isolated, having retreated
into self-made cocoons,
Instead, we need to rally to seek
the Common Good—Summum Bonum.

The Common Good concerns us all.
It presupposes:
Respect for all human persons;
Emancipation of the individual;
Healthy social intercourse;
Our social well-being;
And a just social order.

The Common Good harbors
seeds of a universal social order
conducive to the welfare of
all and sundry.

The Common Good seeks
the progress of nations,
founded on truth, justice and love.

IDENTITY CRISES

Fausse Identité

I do not quite know who I am.
Je ne sais pas au juste qui je suis.
Some call me Anglo;
D'autres m'appellent Froggy.

I still don't know who I am
Je ne sais toujours pas qui je suis.
My name c'est Le Bamenda;
My name is L'Ennemi dans la maison;
My name c'est le Biafrais;
Mon nom is underclass citizen;
My name c'est le maladroit.

Taisez-vous! Shut up!
Don't bother me!
Ne m'embêtez pas!
Don't you know that je suis ici chez moi?
Vous ignorez que I belong here?
I shall fight to my dernier souffle
to forge a real name pour moi-même.
You shall call me Anglofrog!
Vous m'appellerez Franglo!

Shut up! Taisez-vous!
Don't bother me!
Ne m'embêtez pas!
Vous ignorez que I belong here?
Don't you know that je suis ici chez moi?

I shall fight to my last breath
to forge a real lingo for myself.
I'll speak Français;
Je parlerai English
Together we'll speak camfranglais;
C'est-à-dire qu'ensemble,
We'll speak le Camerounisme,
Because ici nous sommes tous chez nous
A bon entendeur salut!
He who has ears should hear!

Disposable Beings

Human trafficking—
The bane of humanity!
Abomination against the human race.
Root cause of the dehumanizing trade?
Greed, materialism, moral decadence—
Main culprits of the infamous trade.
Disposable people coerced into forced labor
On farms, in factories, and in brothels.
The most vulnerable of them all—
Children not spared the indignity.

Sex trafficking—
Perpetrated by *bayam-sellam*[6]
Of human cargo for the profit motive.
Flagrant violation of the Universal
Declaration of Human Rights.
Millions enslaved in the sex industry!
There are more slaves without chains today
Than all the people stolen
From Africa centuries ago!

---

6 vendors

Masquerades

There is no question.
A world of ours is a stage
Where everyone comes to act.
Garbed in multifaceted masks,
Folks make believe in all occupations!

Foes act like friends;
Friends mistaken for foes.
Mortals impersonate immortals;
Humans pass for prima donnas.
Miscreants act the pious.
Self-seekers masquerade as
Selfless philanthropists.
Servants of Satan spot the mask
Of men of God!

Truth is this globe is replete with impostors.
How long shall we dress in borrowed robes?
How long shall we pull the wool
Over the eyes of folks?
How long shall we wear masks?
I call a spade a spade.
Could not care less whose ox is gored!

Tough Love

Black and white in love?
Call off the bluff!
There is no lost love between
Black and White in this
Juneteenth[7] Clime.
A partially blind observer would
Testify that this Joint
Harbors two nations in one.
The one Caucasian;
The other Black.

Black and white in love?
No way!
The racial divide is palpable,
In all the nooks and crannies—
In the workplace;
In houses of worship;
In shopping malls;
In communities of learners;
At bus stops;
In restaurants and taverns;
In places of recreation.

Everywhere
Blacks and whites
Behave like roadside
Strangers seeking shelter from rain
In no man's land,

---

7 Juneteenth, celebrated on June 19, is the name given to emancipation
day by African-Americans. June 19th was shortened to Juneteenth.

Each one waiting anxiously
For the rain to cease
Before they can go their separate ways.
They barely put up with one another.

Manacles

Man is born free,
But in chains everywhere—
Fetters of daily toil;
Chains of substance abuse;
Shackles of social upheaval;
Chains of moral decadence;
Manacles of matrimonial infidelity;
Chains of cerebral ineptitude;
Bonds of fundamentalist bigotry;
Chains of imperialist yoke.
Manacles of rivalry.

Man is born free,
But everywhere entangled—
Shackles of bondage!
Manacles of myopia!
Man is hard at
Work decimating woman.
Womankind is engrossed in the
Eerie task of undoing humankind!
Each passing day portends
Woe for humanity's
Fateful apocalypse.

Sanctimonious Hypocrisy

Apartheid,
You are a monster!
You tear people apart,
Your tongue is fiery
Your lingo hate,
You call us *kaffirs*[8],
You brand us Bushmen,
You think we are dirty *coolies*[9],
However, who are you?
You are the shame of humanity!
Epitome of human bigotry and folly.

Apartheid,
Your God is white,
Your Lucifer black.
Who says white is divine!
Who says black is anathema?
Call off the bluff!
Is your Creator a racist?
Methinks God is colorblind.

Apartheid,
Your creed is racial cleansing.
Yet you are no master of your libido.
You fornicate with our black sisters,
You have coitus with our colored mothers,

8 Term used especially in Southern Africa as a disparaging term for a
Black person.
9 Derogatory term used in Southern Africa for an unskilled laborer
employed cheaply, especially one brought from Asia.

The myriad hybrids in these precincts
Are your handiwork.
You pathological liar!

Apartheid,
Your die is cast!
Bow your head in shame.
We sang requiem for you
In April 1994—
The fateful year for you and your ilk!
You belong in the trashcan of history.
You are a spent force.
Adieu!

Simulacrum

Everyone has the right to life,
Never mind the muggings
And rampant shootings
That have made this the part
Of the globe a war zone!

Everyone has the right
To freedom of expression,
Never mind the tacit press censorship
And journalistic fraud
That have become the hallmark
Of our mass media.

Everyone has the right,
To freedom of worship
Conscience, thought, and belief
Never mind the telltale
Separation of Church and State.

Everyone has the right
To freedom of movement
Never mind the dehumanizing
Searches at our airports
That have made commuting
By air a nightmare!

Everyone has the right
To a clean environment
Never mind the fact that
Our Clean Air Act
Is not worthier than the paper

On which it is written!

Everyone has the right
To adequate housing,
Remember Section 8.[10]
Never mind the many waifs and homeless
That have taken up residence on sidewalks.

Everyone has the right
To good health care,
Never mind the fact that
A sizeable proportion
Of the nation's population
Have no access to health care
On account of inability
To afford health insurance.

Everyone has the right
To inherent dignity
In addition, to have their dignity respected.
Never mind the fact that
Immigrants are on the run
Day in day out within our borders.

Everyone has the right to education,
Never mind the tacit re-segregation
That has become the stock-in-trade

---

10 The Section 8 Rental Voucher Program provides assistance to very low-income households by allowing families to choose privately owned rental housing. The public housing authority (PHA) generally pays the landlord the difference between 30 percent of household income and the PHA-determined payment standard-about 80 to 100 percent of the fair market rent (FMR).

Of our educational system.

Everyone is equal before the law,
Never mind the racial-profiling
That has made some citizens
More equal before the law than others do.

No one may be subjected to slavery,
Never mind the thinly veiled enslavement
That is transpiring in the corporate world.

This is the letter of the law,
Spirit of rule of the law,
Our Bill of Rights is an oxymoron.

Shithole

The populace,
Call you *Palais de l'Unité*
Others christen you Unity Palace.
What a misnomer!
You are a dungeon of disunity.
Beyond your glitter and glamour
Lurk many a machination!
Dog-eat-dog vendetta,
Survival-of-the-fittest recipe
In that shithouse.

The nation still mourns Jean-Irène—
First Lady of blessed memory.
Have you laid her ghost to rest?
Your hands dripping with her blood!
Unashamedly, you picked a *wolowoss*[11]
To step in her shoes!
What became of her twin babies
Fathered by the Abakwa cab driver?
What a shame for the nation!

You stink murder!
You smell incest!
You exude perversion!
Many have perished in your name,
Some incarcerated in mass graves,
Others fed to the Sanaga crocodiles.

---

11 prostitute

Mind you,
Absentee tenant of Etoudi,
He that kills by the sword
Perishes by the sword
That is the law of Karma.

Bootstraps

I have pulled myself up
By my own bootstraps.
Life has not been a bed of roses!
Should I say I'm a self-made man?
Nay, there's no such thing!
In little ways and big ways
people have aided my ascent.
If I've seen further,
It's by standing on the shoulders
of giants, quips the anonymous pundit.
To them I owe a debt of gratitude.

Life has not been a free ride for me,
I've made it by dint of hard work
Should I say I am the lone architect?
Of all my glories?
Should I arrogate to myself
All the successes that have come
My way in life?
Not at all!
Tom, Dick and Harry
Have chipped in their quota
To bring me to the status
In which I find myself.
To all and sundry
I say *na gode*!¹²

---

12 Thank you in the Hausa language!

Orphaned in my teens,
I've had to scrape a bare living
in a bid to reach my goal in life.
Should I beat my chest and say
Down with you who did not fend for me
In my days of gloom?
Absolutely not!

The story of my life runs
like a horror movie.
Should I see myself as a Prima Donna?
No, no! No one can carve out a niche
for himself as a loner.
To all the unsung architects of my life,
I say, *ndoh!*[13]

---

13 Thanks in the Bamunka language.

Diploma Mills

Bow your head in shame!
Fraudster!
Custodian of bogus diplomas.
Graduate of the University of Bonamusadi.
How do you feel in your
Counterfeit Academic robes?
Comfortable? Ill at ease?

Shame onto you!
Owner of fake certificates.
Alumni of the Academy of Feymania.
You've thrown your pride to the dogs.
Prisoner of your own conscience.

Hang your head in disgrace!
Intellectual charlatan!
You trade degrees for sex.
Tell us about your sexually
transmitted *license ès lettres*.[14]

Pseudo-intellectual!
Your university is the shopping mall
Where you haggle for the cost of degrees.
Liberate yourself from self-imposed incarceration.
Dispose of your ill-acquired qualifications.
Begin from scratch and ride toward mental freedom.
That is purgative.

NOMENCLATURAL MUSINGS

Nom De Plume

The euphoria is nondescript!
I am at a loss for words.
I search for words to describe
The glee that fills me
each time my nom de plume
appears in print.
I write therefore I am.

The mirth is indescribable!
It's a renewed feeling of joy
that floods my heart of hearts
each moment I catch sight of my
Pen-name in print.
I write therefore I am.

I am in the seventh heaven
each day I spot in print a line
Or verse of mine in print—
figment of my imagination.
Triumph of the acceptance slip
over the rejection note.
I write therefore I am.

Money sharks
may count their treasure
in gold and diamond.
I count my wealth
In intellectual baggage.
I write therefore I am.

Nomenclature

There is nothing more important
Than a person's name.
The problem is we toy around with names.
People no long use their real names!
We take liberties with nomenclature:

Elizabeth has become Beth;
Susan has metamorphosed into Sue;
Patricia has been reborn Pat or Patty;
Christopher has been transformed into Chris;
Michael is Mike.

Charles is Chuck,
Peter is Pete,
And the list continues.
Why are we doing this?
We make others feel
Like human counterfeits!

Do you know what's done
To people who have tongue-twisters
Like Mr. Chokolokobangushia?
We ignore them altogether.
Isn't that smart?

People's names are their most
Valued assets from birth,
We have no leeway cart
Trifle with people's names!

Nurture

The nature and nurture drumbeat rolls on.
Humans learn by half-and-half—
Partly by nature;
Partly by nurture,
Quips Charles Darwin and cohorts.

This is the rationale
For proper parenting.
The family is society in miniature.
A badly nurtured kid
Is anathema to society?

Like a tender plant,
An offspring is desirous
Of nurture from the cradle.
To posit that a child
Would mature into a man unattended
Is tantamount to self-delusion.

A kid left to its own devices
Is like a drowning man
Without a life jacket
Abandoned in mid-stream.
To fend for himself.

Straddling The Mungo

I no care if you be Francophone,
I no care if you be Anglophone,
I no even mind for youa tribe,
I no mind for youa *kanda*.[14]
I mean de color for youa skin.

Wheda[15] you be Graffi or you be Nkwah,
Wheda you be Bakweri or you be Banwa,
Wheda you be Bassa or you be Ewondo,
Wheda you be Bororo or you be Hausa ,
Na daso one ting get use for we skin.
And dat ting na blood.

If you cot ma skin,
And I cot you skin,
Na daso one ting go comot,
And dat ting na blood.
And di color for dat blood
na red for all man.

So mek we no begin knack skin,
We go die di same.
All we na grong kaku.

---

14 skin
15 whether

Rape of the Classroom

Bogus is the epithet I've elected to employ
To qualify certain self-styled
Teachers in our milieu.

Teachers of bygone times
Perceived instruction as a vocation.
Not anymore!

For want of a better livelihood,
Some charlatans have strayed
Into the noble profession.

Brand them checkbook instructors.
They have no other aspiration
Beyond making a quick buck.

How many times have I seen?
These impostors stagger
Into the classroom, stinking like breweries?

How often has one surprised
These hacks fornicating with students
Without an iota of shame?

How many times have they cooked the books
In an attempt to hide backlog,
And dissimulate counterfeit qualifications?

Tell me that not every teacher is spurious,
I challenge you to show me an upright one,
And Sodom and Gomorrah will be spared.

Rat Race

What hurry and flurry!
Our world is locked in an infernal race.
Joggling for power,
Scheming for fortune,
Wheeling and dealing!

In this rat race,
Water is thicker than blood!
Sister rises against brother,
Brother stands against sister.

In this rat race,
Husband deals deathblows to wife,
Children undercut parents.
There is fire and brimstone.

A veritable rat race,
Humanity has metaphorphosed into a zoo.
Humans have become beasts and
Love has been transformed into hate.

Harambe[16]

I do sing renaissance—
African renaissance.
Our newfound buzzword.
Dilettantism or panacea?
That is the cause of disagreement.

We are all engulfed,
In the claws of a notorious monster-
The penchant for borrowed code-names.
How come we prescribe alien remedies
For homebred maladies?
How does communalism resonate?
In lieu of renaissance?

Call it Ubuntu,
Christen it Harambe if you like,
That's what I sing—
Unwavering communal spirit.
Harambe frees the mind,
It forges ahead.
That is why I chant Harambe,
That is why I sing Ubuntu.

---

16 Working together for freedom; communal labor

Requiem for Love

Love has passed away,
Let us not talk about her anymore.
She died ere long!
Trivialized in infancy and choked
To death by promiscuity.

Love has given up the ghost,
Unable to bear the weight of infidelity.
Incapable of resisting the temptation of lust.
She died ages ago.
Let us wear sackcloth,
In addition, smear our faces with
Ashes to commemorate her passing.

Lexicographers would do well
To delete LOVE form their lexicons
Because she died a long time ago.
Love is devoid of meaning in this day and time,
Love is dead.

Mange-Mille[17]

Flatfoot[18]
Mere khaki![19]
We give you the fatigues,
We give you the gun,
You have the baton as well,
To protect us,
Not to molest us,
Yet you are our worst enemy!

You deflower our virgins,
You defile our mothers,
You harass the innocent,
You spare the culprit,
What became of the court docket?
You dissimulated it!
What happened to the dope dealer?
You colluded with him!
Where is the bank robber?
You aided and abetted his escape,
You are a rogue cop!

The bank is your target,
The supermarket another lure,
The cash-in-transit tempts you,
You are a rogue cop!

---

17 Police officer who takes bribes from commuters
18 Slang for police officer
19 Policeman

The commuter industry is ablaze,
You stand on the sidelines, why?
Maybe you have a thing at stake.
Do you own a taxi enterprise?
You are a rogue cop!

How long must we bear with you?
How long must we overlook your roguery?
Our safety and security is your job,
We pay for it.
Do the right thing,
And do it now!

PENMANSHIP

Plume

I write what I like.
Writers are born;
And not made.
That's a tall tale!
He that has nothing to say,
Cannot write,
Quips Bernard Shaw.

Penmanship,
Like all walks of like,
Calls for systematic apprenticeship.
It has nothing to do with hacking.
It does not tally with plagiarism.
It's a figment of one's imagination.
I write what I like.

I write verse therefore I am.
Poetry is not dead wood
as many are wont to believe.
Verse is a vehicle for the
transportation of mixed emotions.

Poets create their own world;
a world as it should be.
Poetry stands for a worldview.

Poetry fulfils myriad social functions:
How reverent the lyrics of our Anthem!
Isn't that poetry too?
How soul-searching the melody of our hymnals!

Isn't that poetry too?
How captivating our rhymed commercials!
That too is poetry.
Poetry is not dead wood.
Vive la poésie![20]
I write what I like.

Predator

It boggles the mind
To think that Man
Is the vilest homo sapien
That God ever created.

It beats logic to fathom
That Man is Man's predator.
Take a walk down memory lane.
Ponder the brutal assassination
Of former Pakistani Prime Minister,
Benazir Bhutto by a suicide bomber.

Avail yourself of hindsight,
Revisit the Jewish Holocaust,
Handiwork of Adolf Hitler,
Brain behind demonic Nazism.

Have a flashback,
Rethink the brutality of
Hiroshima and Nagasaki
Relive the bloodbath.

Recall Verwoerdian South Africa,
Bastion of sanctimonious hypocrisy
Locus of cosmetic social tinkering:
The Sharpeville Massacre;
The Soweto Uprising and aftermath.

Recall the Rwandan Genocide,
Mutual decimation of Hutu and Tutsi.

Don't forget the infamous Darfur genocide
that caused John Karang his life.

Recall neo-nazis,
The likes of Milosevic and ilk.
All these bear testimony
To man's inhumanity to man.

Rap on the Venal

Graft,
Tchoko,[21]
The bane of our nation,
Spook in the wheel of nation-building.

I smell corruption everywhere,
I sniff nepotism around,
I see it in all nooks and crannies,
Canker of the homeland.

Everywhere,
Nepotism reigns supreme,
Cronyism the national creed,
Mediocrity recompensed;
Virtuosity penalized,
What a load of ironies!

The *père de la nation*[22] relishes kickbacks,
The *planton*[23] wants *un petit quelque chose*[24],
The *mbere*[25] takes bribes,
The *zangalewa*[26] accepts gratification,
The *gendarme*[27] aids and abets corruption.
What a legacy for posterity!

---

21 Bribe
22 Head of state
23 Office messenger
24 Small bribe
25 Policeman
26 soldier
27 Police in francophone African countries

Phallus

Phallus,
Friend or foe?
That is the question!
Source of many a woe and bliss.

Phallus,
Modicum of the anatomy,
Yet cause of all the world's woes.
Consider the Monica Lewinsky sex scandal.

Phallus,
Storehouse of libido.
Ponder the Pedophilia scandal
In the Roman Catholic Church.

Penile terrorist!
Help! S.O.S!
Procure me an antidote!
It's either that or
Outright castration.

Time Bomb

In coitus,
The pleasure is fleeting,
The posture ludicrous,
The cost exorbitant,
Quips the Sage.

Our country's top sport is sex!
The game that's most relished
By the young and the not-so-young
Is sexual intercourse.

Admonish them on th*e prevalence*
Of the dog sickness[28]
They will scoff at you and remind you
That AIDS is nothing but an
Afro Invention to Discourage Sex.

Yet folks are dropping dead like flies,
Graves are full of young men and women
Who ought to be alive and strong.
There is no more land to bury the dead.
Mortuaries are full to the brim!

Are we nymphomaniacs?
Or sex daredevils?
Are we 7+1 agnostics?
Truth of the matter is:
We are sitting on a time bomb.

---

28 AIDS

Impunity

How long
Shall we turn a blind eye
To the crime and grime of our society?

How long
Shall we feign ignorance
Of the decadence that's eating
Deep into the moral fabric
Of our community?

How long
Shall we not care fig about
The endemic poverty that
Has become our bedfellow?

How long
Shall we not give a damn to
The fact that our roads are death-tracks?

How long
Shall we pretend not to see
The siphoning of our natural resources
By erstwhile colonial masters?

How long
Shall we stay mute?
In the face of wanton abuse
Of the populace by belly-politicians?

How long
Shall we overlook
The fact that tribalism
Is our national leprosy?

How long
Shall we make believe
That when Yaoundé breathes
La nation se porte bien29

How long
Shall we delude ourselves
That the end justifies the means.

How long
Shall we continue?
To live in a neo-colonial fool's paradise?

How long
Shall we continue?
To offer our nation
To the highest bidder?

How long
Shall we not see that?
Fogies and Anglos
Are wrapped in a bond
Of mutual distrust in Amazonia?
How long?

---

29 The nation is faring well.

Ntarikon

In that fateful year 1990,
The *kanas*[30] man of Ntarikon,
Ni John Fru Ndi
Stuck out his neck in defiance
Of the junta in Yaoundé.
Resistance is defiance.

Amidst elephantine opposition,
masterminded by the Beti-led
pseudo-government in Ngola,
the Social Democratic Front,
Mbiya Mbivodo's political albatross
Saw the light of day in Abakwa.
Resistance is defiance.

The aftermath of the heroic venture
Was macabre and sinister:
Myriads perished in cold blood,
Hundreds savaged and raped.
All kept a stiff upper lip.
Resistance is defiance.

Many more sodomized and brutalized
By gun-totting lunatics
In military fatigues.
Countless tara31 and complice[32]

---

30 testicles; courage
31 individuals
32 comrade

Rounded up in matango[33]
And matutu[34] taverns in swine quarter
Ended up in the infamous BMM—
Brigade Mixte Mobile up-station.
Bamenda pikin chopped fire[35]
In the face of tyranny.
Resistance is defiance.

Weep not Ni John!
We will overcome!
Your sweat did not ooze in vain.
Some brand you sell-out,
Others say you've eaten soya[36],
Many claim you have dined
With the Gaullist Mammon
Give them the lie!
Friends and foes may croak,
Le chien aboie la caravane passe[37].
Resistance is defiance.

Falter not brother John!
Freedom shall be ours,
come rain come thunder!
The liberation of your brethren
West of the Mungo River
Shall be the ultimate victory
Fear not brother!
Cowards die many times

---

33 palm wine
34 raphia wine
35 children of Bamenda
36 Others say you have struck a deal with the enemy
37 The dog barks as the caravan goes by.

Before their real death
Resistance is defiance.

Veneer of Piety

You don the cassock
And swear by the Bible;
Yet you wheel and deal with
the *ngambe*[38] man from Oku.
Travesty of religiosity!

You preach from the pulpit,
And brand yourself born-again;
Yet you commune with the *feyman*[39]
And do business with the *money-doubler*[40].
Veneer of piety!

You tell the beads,
And peruse the Koran,
You hit your forehead on the ground,
And pray five times a day.
You've been to Mecca and back;
Yet you collude with
Men of the underworld.
Sanctimonious hypocrisy!

Fool not yourself!
God's omnipresent,
He's omniscient,
God's omnipotent.
The day of reckoning is at hand.
When that day comes,

---

38 fortune-teller
39 conman
40 counterfeiter

There will be gnashing
And grinding of teeth.
For each man shall have
his tale to tell.

Vicious Circle

Slaves of yesterday;
Masters of today.
The infernal cycle knows no end.

Colonized of the past;
Neo-colonizers of the present.
The wheel of fortune swings.

Underdogs of yesteryears;
Overlords of the moment.
What goes around comes around.

The lure remains predictable,
The profit motive strong,
Cloaked in a semblance of philanthropy.

The imperialist venture
dons the fake nomenclature
of civilizing-mission.

Pray, who's civilizing who?
Remember the Nile Valley?
Cradle of civilization!

Remember Timbuktu?
Seat of black erudition!
Cease pulling the wool!

Remember Songhai?
Ivory tower of negro academe.
Remember Mali Empire?
Who's civilizing who?

Phantoms!

At first sight I thought
they were phantoms!
Then I persuaded myself they
were perambulating cadavers.

A great many Evas are starving
to death in the name of weight-watching!
They've fallen victim to terminal anorexia—
Morbid fear of having any padding on the bones.

Ergo, many peck at their meals,
Others gulp down slimming concoctions,
Many more drink fortified wines and spirits,
Others snort cocaine and smoke marijuana.

Surely there's beauty in Divine handiwork.
Wherefore this craving to be as thin as wafers?
Where comes this urge to be skeletal?
When shall we be free from the tyranny of self-rejection?

Trappings of Royalty

Divine rights of kings!
Did I hear that?
I loathe monarchy!
What with its autocratic
trappings of power,
All antithetical to the
precepts of democracy?

How dare you arrogate
divinity to your mortal selves?
Showcase of royal conceit!
Kings,
Queens,
Fons,
Chiefs,
Princes,
Princesses,
Notorious rapists
of inalienable rights.

You hold *nchindas*[41]
Captive in perpetuity.
You erect harems replete
With *ntoh wontoh*[42] held in bondage.
You misappropriate tribal land,
And glorify self-succession.

---

41 Royal pages
42 Royal wives

Gone are the days of autocracy!
Bygone are the *suns*[43] of ultra-traditionalists!
Away with royal power!
Down with monarchical authority!

---

43 Era

The Tremor

March 28th, that telltale date.
The chariots of the gods
of Mt Fako spate fire,
metamorphosing into an inferno.
The eruption rocked the very foundations
Of Cameroon's tallest peak.

Faced with the onslaught
of ferocious red hot lava,
residents of Buea and its environs
lost countenance and fled
in various directions.

Kitchen utensils dropped from pantries,
Clothes flew out of wardrobes,
Wailing trees bent double,
Stark naked victims scampered helter-skelter,
As the cannibalistic lava
threatened to engulf their homes.

It's strange, very strange indeed
how humans are quick to shed
all trappings of rank and status
in the face of a calamity.

On that day,
There was no difference
between the governor
and his office messenger;
There was no distinction

between the police commissioner
and a *gardien de la paix*[44];
there was no disparity
between the bayam sellam
and the court clerk;
The *bendskin*[45] driver
and the *pousse-pousse*[46] man
were the same in the boat,
fleeing from a common foe.

The genesis of the quake
remains unknown to date.
Blaming the ire of the gods,
local chieftains poured libation,
and sacrificed goats and sheep
in a bid to placate ancestral spirits.
To no avail!

Puny efforts made by volcanic pundits
flown in from France proved futile
in the attempt to unravel
the cause of the oddity.
Patent proof that God's ways are uncanny.

44Police constable
45 Motorcycle
46 Wheel-cart

Necromancy

Concocted in heathen laboratories,
You passed off as indigenous science.
Yet you are the bane of humanity.
Your macabre deeds legion;
permeating all the nooks
and crannies of the globe.

People call you *juju*,
Some call you *famla*,
Others brand you *magan*,
Many christen you *tobassi*.
I call you *gris-gris*

What's in a name?
Truth of the matter,
You are our arch-enemy!

In your name,
Families are torn asunder.
In your name,
The elderly kill the young.
In your name,
The young brutalize the old.
In your name,
Houses are torched at random.
In your name,
Kangaroo courts judge the innocent.
In your name,
The law is flouted with impunity.

Witchcraft,
You set parents against offspring.
Through you,
The evil-minded wreak havoc,
Sibling rises against sibling,
You pit friend against friend.

Witchcraft,
You're a stumbling to social harmony.
It's high time we bade you farewell.

Soccer Mania

Rendezvous of sports maniacs.
You glitter with glory,
Through you,
Many a sportsman and woman
Earn a ticket into the hall of fame.
You nurture stars in the cradle of stardom.

Yet your glory is but vainglory!
You occasion substance abuse,
Cut-throat competition,
Your stock-in-trade.
Double standards,
Your modus operandi.

Through you,
Perverts wreak vengeance—
Remember the Honduras/El Salvador Vendetta in 1969?
Recall the England/Tunisia do-or-die encounter in 1998?
Don't forget the machinations that surrounded
South Africa's bid for hosting the World Cup in 2006.
Methinks you're the shame of sportsmanship,
The very epitome of make-believe.

World cup,
Poles apart with justice,
Hard to locate your much-vaunted fairness.
Rainbow assembly torn apart
By thinly veiled segregation.
The bane of genuine stardom.

Casket

Had I known
that one day I will return
to dust as naked as an earth worm,
I'd not be supercilious.

Had I known
that in death there are no greater beings,
I'd not be vainglorious.

Had I known
that there's no room in death
for my ill-gotten wealth,
I' d not be materialistic.

Had I known
that in death there's no status,
I'd be not be chauvinistic.

Had I known
that in death there are no races,
I'd not be a racist.

Had I known
that death makes NO distinction
between the black man and the white man,
I'd not be a supremacist.

When all is said and done,
I now know that
death comes to all and sundry
in the same manner—SLUMBER.
In death there is eternal freedom.

Requiem!

In those good old days
when square pegs did not
stand in round holes,
a degree earned at university
was a ticket to prosperity.
Not any more!
These are the *suns* of the New Deal—
The reign of mediocrity.

In those good old days
when merit had meaning,
One could climb the social ladder
by dint of hard work.
Not anymore!
This is the dawn of the Raw Deal—
The reign of *man-know-man-*
The era of you-scratch-my-back
I-scratch-your-own.

In this day and time,
nothing goes for nothing—
If you desire something,
You grease the palm.
It's the reign of collusion.

In this day and time,
if you're desirous of success,
you'd better found yourself a godfather
This is the age of bribery and corruption.
Sing requiem for meritocracy!

Vantage Point

Life may be a bed of roses to you;
To me it's a long haul.
It all depends on vantage point.

Wealth may mean materialism to you;
To me it's rich spirituality.
It all depends on vantage point.

Religion may be opium of the poor to you;
To me it's conscious self-recognition
It all depends on vantage point.

You may find solace in substance abuse;
To me addiction is tantamount to self-destruction.
It all depends on vantage point.

Your *savoir-vivre*[47] may be--
A tooth for a tooth
And an eye for an eye.

To me it's give to Caesar what's Caesar's
And to God what's God's.
It all depends on vantage point.

---

47 Way of life

Taxi Driver Wisdom

The game of politics
obeys the same rule in the
West, East, South, and North—
Line your pockets as fast
as possible before it's too late.

All politicians have one creed—
Do whatever it takes to
hang onto power in perpetuity,
even if it means throwing
conscience to the dogs.

All politicians are multicolored—
Veritable chameleons,
varying colors to tally with
auspicious circumstances.

A politician fallen
from grace to grass
is like a wounded lion.
He'll stop at nothing
in his quest for vengeance.

When all is said and done,
a good politician is (s)he
that is dead and buried.

Crazy Love

Love is a precious thing.
True love is a pearl.
It has remarkable attributes—
True Love is kind;
It is patient.
True Love is not envious;
It is not jealous.
True Love is humble;
It is not boastful.
True Love is selfless;
It is not self-seeking.
True Love is slow to anger.
It is not vindictive;
It doesn't keep a
record of wrongs.
True love does not delight
in falsehood;
It cherishes truth.
True Love protects always;
It trusts at all times;
It preserves always.
Never underestimate
the liberating power of true love.

PHANTOMS

Fads

Life's a fad
Think of racism:
compulsive hatred
of other races.

Life's a fad
Think of fanaticism:
compulsive enthusiasm
for one's idol.

Life's a fad
Think of fascism:
compulsive authoritarian views.

Life's a fad
Think of nihilism:
compulsive rejection of
religious and moral principles.

Life's a fad
Think of jingoism:
compulsive bellicosity.

Life's a fad
Think of chauvinism:
compulsive prejudice
against the fair sex.

Life's a fad
Think of Pedophilia:

compulsive sexual obsession
directed toward kids.

Life' a fad
Think of dipsomania:
compulsive craving for liquor.

Life's a fad
Think of nymphomania:
compulsive sexual
desire in women.

Life's a fad
Think of misogyny:
compulsive dislike for women.

Life's a fad
Think of misogamy:
compulsive aversion for marriage.

Life's a fad
Think of misanthropy:
compulsive hatred of
Human-kind.

Truly
This life of ours
is nothing but a huge fad!

Rate Race

Time is pregnant with meaning—
Time and tide wait for no one,
A stitch in time saves nine,
Procrastination is the thief of time.
There's time for everything:
Time to work and time to rest.

In bread-and-butter world,
Time is money--
Modus operandi for capital-mongers.
Humanity and time are locked
in a vicious race headed for nowhere.

Folks can't eat anymore!
Folks can't rest anymore!
Man no rest, day de go mandat de bole![48]
Folks can't play anymore!
Folks can't commune anymore!
Time's become an over-bearing master!

Homes are ripped asunder--
Parents vie with one another
for mundane wealth.
Children left to their own devices have
the leeway to do to their heart's content.
I wonder if this infernal
race will ever come to an end.

---

48 No time to rest, our days are numbered.

RAPE OF DEMOCRACY

Demo-Crazy

In these precincts,
Polls are seldom a litmus test
for popular mandate.

Benefiting from the privilege
of incumbency the powers-that-be
make a sham of fair and free elections—

Ballot boxes filled with
ballot papers prior to election day,
Ghost polling-stations set up in fons'palaces,
And in the private homes of friends
to the Ruling party,
Rassemblement Démagogique du Peuple Camerounais
(RDPC)[49]
Electoral gerrymandering knows not bounds.

The legislature transformed
into a rubberstamp;
The judiciary reduced to the posture
of toothless bulldog;
The execute lords it over
by fair means and foul!

For these reasons and more,
international election monitors
have christened our brand
Of democracy brazen demagoguery!

---

49 Cameroon Peoples' Demagogic Party (C.P.D.M.)

I am head and toes in a crusade.
These verses that you peruse
are my lethal ammunition
against a cancerous society.

I am unfazed by all odds.
These verses that you read
are an outburst of bitter
emotions against an amoral society.
They're mightier than the sword!

I am steeped in a crusade.
These lines that you pore
over at this point in time
are a figment of my imagination.
I am primed for the vendetta
against a venal society.
Ere long, there'll be an onslaught!

Je Wanda

Il y a quelque chose que
Je wanda depuis from,
If par hazard, I say par hasard
Because le locataire d'Etoudi
Ne croit aucunément in the truth of this dictum:
"From dust you came, and to dust you shall return."

Anyhow, si le mandat de Paul Biya parvient à bolè
That be say, il crève bon gré mal gré,
Who will take his place as père de la nation?
Je wanda seulement et je sabi que
Beaucoup de camers wanda comme moi.
Est-que je dis vrai ou non?

Don't forget that la relève ne
Se prépare pas au Cameroun, hein.
Si Biya crève today, certainement que
Son mandat va bolè un jour, fais quoi fait quoi,
Est-ce que na that garçon de courses
Que vous appelez Cavayé Yéguié Djibril,

Rejeton des parents kirdi from Mada
In the Mayo Sara arrondissement,
Na yi go chop chia ou alors
C'est le soi-disant président du Sénat fantôme
That does not exist qui va squatter à Etoudi
Until further notice, Je wanda seulement?

De toutes les facons, we no wan
See zangalewa for Etoudi si
Popol parvient à crever for better or for worse!
L'Ongola mérite mieux que les zangalewa half-book
Dem go come nous foutre le bordel
Partout dans le bled.

Chiba

J'accuse les politiquarts cameriens
D'être non seulement mboutoucous
But en même temps des feymans.
Je les accuse tous—opposants et Rdépécistes
Because ils ne font que pratiquer la belly politics.

J'accuse les tontons macoutes ongolais
Etant donné que dem don ton be na
Les vampires de la République.
Mola, langua-moi!
Comment toi même tu nyè cette aff, no?

Est-ce ma tchat c'est seulement le sissia?
Whether na Paul Biya
Or c'est Ni John Fru Ndi, ou Ndam Njoya,
N'est-ce pas eux tous, ils mangent le même soya?
How you check say dem fit tok true tok?

Vraiment, où est la différence,
 Que ce soit Popol ou l'originaire de Ntarikon à Etoudi,
N'est-ce pas dem all na kick pipo?
Na wa for dis we own kondre-o!
Nos politiquarts nous font voir kan-kan wahala.

J' accuse les politiquarts ongolais
Because ils sont tous les kickmans,
Transformés en élus du peuple.
Je veux qu'on les foute tous en taule
Yes mbombo, dat be say dem must yua ngata!

We don tok! One day one day
Ali Baba et ses quarante voleurs
Must yua ngata, sans oublier le bao locataire
Du quat du peuple à Etoudi
Because Popol sep sep na popo Kengué.

Chief Inoni

Popo me, I di askam sey hein,
Da we own Massa Inoni,
What was he at Etoudi? Hein?
Chinda or Djimtété?
Je wanda seulement,hein!

Chief Inoni Ephraim
Si hier tu es en haut,
And auday tu es en bas,
Dat wan mean say weti, hein?
Je wanda seulement,hein!

Chief Inoni Ephraim
Achouka ngongoli for check sey you be frog!
Au fait, me I di askam say hein,
Ce Massa Inoni il était même quoi au palais d'Etoudi?
Planton, nchinda ou chef de terre?

Chief Inoni Ephraim
Aschouka for mimba sey
Etoudi na youa own chasse gardée!
Et ton role dans l'affaire Albatros?
Did you have a hand in it or not?

Ou alors tu n'es qu'un bouc émissaire
Comme les autres malheureux.
Les Camers know ce qu'il s'est passé
Avec les mbourous de l'ancien chaud gars,
Chef forever and ever du palais d'Etoudi.

Chief Inoni Ephraim
Achouka ngongoli!
Today, te voilà alors en train de crever
Dans les ténèbres de Kondengui
Way no man no sabi pourquoi.

A qui alors la faute? A toi ou à Popol?
Cheh! Le Cameroun c'est le Cameroun!
Mais au lieu de garder son tchinda dans la taule
A perpétuité better Popol dis à Massa Inoni
To back da dos et retrouver sa liberté provisoire!

Si Chief Inani dit non
Son mandat va bolè à Kondengui
Car qui vole un oeuf, vole un boeuf.
Famille-o! Famille! Comment vous-mêmes
Vous nyè ce tchat no?

Guide Eclairé

Grand Camarade, El Hajj
Je check say nous tous on le know.
Ce dictateur qui avait foutu le Cameroun
En l'air avant de donner
Son chia à son nchinda—ancien chaud gars.
Ce bandit beti qui plume le Cameroun à vue d'oeil.

Il est bien vrai que les politiquarts
Sont one and the same partout sur notre planète.
C'est même pour cela que je wanda
Au sujet des dépouilles du Grand Camarade,
Abandonnées à Dakar depuis from.
Why must Ahijdo's remains stay in Dakar?

Je wanda surtout why Popol
N'a pas utilisé son number six pour
Fait venir la carcasse de ce pauvre
Musulman whey yi been dash yi chia.
Pourquoi ne pas ramener ses dépouilles
Ne serait-ce que pour calmer les esprits troublés?

Il y a des taras qui nous remplissent
Les oreilles avec leur ntamulung choir
Selon lequel Grand Camarade fut
Un meilleur kamambrou que Popol
Je leur tok carrément de shut up,
Parce qu'ils ne savent rien de ce qu'ils langua.

Ces mbombos n'ont qu'à aller tchatcher avec
Les baos comme Reuben Um Nyobé,

Ernest Ouandié, Félix Moumié, Albert Ndongmo,
Albert Womah Mukong et Wambo le Courant,
And then dem go sabi pourquoi je check say
Grand Camarade était un diable comme les autres.

Au vu de ces choses
Faudrait-il peut-être langua que
Un bon politiquart na daso
De one way yi don meng,
Autrement dit, il faut être cadavéré
Pour être un bon politiquart.

Mola, how you sep you nyè dis palava no?
Les camers plenty ont tchatté à Mbiya que,
Non, non et non, vous ne pouvez pas
Abandonner l'ancien kamambrou ça
Dans une piètre sépulture dans un quat étranger.
Soyons sérieux! 6 avril ou non.

Même so, Popo reste impertubable
Hanté comme il est
By the ghost of Grand Camarade.
Il ne veut carrément ya nothing
A propos de cette affaire vachement politisée.
Les appels sont tombés sur les deaf ears!

Dommage au Grand Camarade
Qui n'a jamais pas pris le temps de bien connaître
Le mec Beti à qui il avait largué son chia,
Ce scélérat connu sous le nom de Paul Biya.
Je dirais donc au Grand Camarade, Achouka !

Chairman

Quand on est vieux,
On est vieux no be so?
Le pouvoir appartient
A ceux qui se lèvent tôt.
Laissez-moi tchatcher la vérité à Fru Ndi.

If you want say make some man
Gee chance for road, you sep must
Learn for gee chance for road
For some other mola
Wey yi dey for youa back.

The truth of the matter be say,
Charity begins at home.
We be di check say sometime
Chairman go gee chance for some jeune talent
Make yi corriger Pa Pol.

But sep so, Pa for Ntarikon say
Ngumba must cry for Etoudi,
Yi say Ngumba close must enter Palais.
Ah ah, Je wanda que depuis 1990
This vieux capable don be katika
For SDF jusqu'ai ce jour!

Time waits for nobody
If we want make some man for gee
Chance for road, we sep must
Learn for gee chance for ala man
Way yi day for we back.

Mami Wata

Chantal Pulchérie Vigouroux Biya,
La belle de la République
Ou mami wata qui bouffe
Les mbourous de notre cher pays?

This nkane elle est même quoi?
La mami wata de la République
Ou bien notre première dame?
Je wanda seulement-o
Because si vraiment elle est notre first lady

Pourquoi alors elle sape
Comme une vraie wolowoss?
Est-ce seulement pour attirer
Les yos et les jeunes talents
Etant donné que son ancien chaud gars

Is no longer très chaud?
Ekié! Je wanda only.
Ou alors c'est pour show off tout court
Comme c'est le petit modèle des metoches?
Nous voulons sabi quand même.

Chantal Pulchérie Vigouroux Biya,
Avec le nkap du peuple camerounais
Qu'elle a kick de la caisse noire d'Etoudi,
Elle est devenue mami wata, mini minor
On top of being notre première dame!

C'est Popol qui a cherché
And he don trouva
Just now he must supporta
And for dat supporta
Il faut se méfier car la femme qui a connu la rue…

Coup d'état

Stop the steal!
They chanted!
Armed to the teeth,
Headed for the Capitol,
On January 6, 2021
Baying for Pence's head!

Stop the steal!
They vociferated!
Who were they?
Civilians or Armed Yankees?
What was amiss?

Stop the steal!
They hollered!
Who were they?
Active duty zangalewa
And a few dirt-bags.

Stop the steal!
They fumed.
What was the motive
Behind this hullaballoo?
Coup d'Etat or civil unrest?

Stop the steal!
They ranted!
Who were they?
Trumpists or Rabble-rousers?
Time alone will tell.